Don't Come the Raw Prawn
The Aussie Phrase Dictionary

About the Author

Born into a working-class Melbourne family in 1947, John Blackman started his career in show business in 1969. Since then he has become well-known through radio shows on 2CA, 2GN, 2UE, 2GB, 3AW, 3AK and 3UZ. He has been with Channel Nine's top-rating television show 'Hey Hey It's Saturday' since its inception some twenty years ago and is famous for his laconic sardonic asides and as the voice and brains behind the rascally Dickie Knee.

He is married with one daughter and lives in Melbourne.

To Ronnie,

With all our love and best wishes for the future. From.

Vera and Malcolm Ruediger

Also by John Blackman in Sun
THE AUSSIE SLANG DICTIONARY

DON'T COME THE RAW PRAWN!

JOHN BLACKMAN

SUN
AUSTRALIA

First published 1991 by Pan Macmillan Publishers Australia
a division of Pan Macmillan (Australia) Pty Limited
63–71 Balfour Street, Chippendale, Sydney
A.C.N. 001 184 014
Reprinted 1991

National Library of Australia
cataloguing-in-publication data:
Blackman, John.
    Don't come the raw prawn: the Aussie phrase
    dictionary.
    ISBN 0 7251 0685 9.
    1. Australianisms—Dictionaries. 2. English language
    —Australia—Humor. I. Title.

427.994

Typeset in 11/13pt Souvenir Light by Midland Typesetters
Printed in Australia by Australian Print Group

A Word From John Blackman

After my first book, *The Australian Slang Dictionary*, sold out and reprinted twice, I was convinced of the world's insatiable thirst for more knowledge of our unique and quirky language. Hence this subsequent tome, *Don't Come the Raw Prawn*, the result of months of painstaking (but enjoyable) research which still only scratches the surface of the rich lode of Australian colloquialisms.

Indeed, purists might observe there are some words and phrases missing. You will, however, find many of them in my first publication. (I suspect this is a devious ploy by my publishers to get you to buy both books!)

My extensive research indicates there is still enough raw material available virtually to double the size of this publication but, in the interests of space and economy, I have selected phrases I regard as relevant to today's Aussie lifestyle.

I have not only defined traditional expressions but also introduced some contemporary and local terminology that you may not be familiar with due to geographical or cultural differences.

And once again, where words fail, brilliant young cartoonist Andrew Fyfe has let his dark, fertile mind run rife in illustrations featuring a bloke bearing an uncanny resemblance to myself (legal action pending).

Anyhow, I hope you (and friends, relatives and business associates overseas) enjoy our latest effort and trust you will also have fun colouring in the pictures.

Happy reading!

to put the acid on

acid, to put the . . . on

To ask someone for either help, sex or money. (Some of my friends use sulphuric!)

acre

Your backside. Nothing better than sitting on your acre doing nothing.

Adrians

Abbreviated name of Adrian Quist (the famous tennis player) and rhyming slang for 'pissed' or drunk. How drunk? All I remember is falling asleep as soon as my head hit the accelerator!

aerial ping pong

Derogatory term used by Rugby fans to describe Aussie Rules.

aleck

A person of limited mental capacity who goes through life achieving very little. He (or she) is said to be 'alecking around'.

Alice, the

Abbreviation for famous outback town of Alice Springs. If you say you've just spent the weekend in Alice, you need not be classed as a sex maniac.

alkie

Abbreviation for alcoholic. My doctor asked me how long I could go without a drink and I told him about two blocks.

alley

A marble, sometimes known as 'agate'. If you cop a kick in the agates, it will certainly make your eyes water!

arf-a-mo

No, not Roy Rene's brother Arthur. What we say when we want someone to wait a moment—half a moment! But enough about my sex life, let's move on to the next word.

arse over tit

(1) arse

Buttocks, posterior, your acre.

(2) arse

Uncanny good luck.

(3) arse, given the

If this happens, you are unemployed. Still, the best thing about being unemployed is, each morning when you get up, you're already at work!

(4) arse, to give it the

To throw something useless out.

(5) arse about, to

To mess around with little or no purpose.

(6) arse about face

Back-to-front.

(7) arse over tit

Upside-down.

(8) arse, get your . . . into gear

Get yourself organised.

(9) arse beats class

Generally said to someone who gets a break more through luck than ability.

(10) arsey

Lucky.

Arthur or Martha, doesn't know if he's (or she's)

In these days of sex-change ops, I'm not surprised. A very confused person. My wife had a sex change—now it's Wednesdays and Saturdays instead of Tuesdays and Fridays!

ashtray, as useful as an . . . on a motorbike

Totally useless. About the same as a waterproof tea bag.

Australian adjective, the great

Euphemism used before we could say 'bloody' with relative impunity. These days, it's even used in a drink/drive advertising campaign in Victoria. 'If you drink, then drive, you're a bloody idiot!'

doesn't know if he's Arthur or Martha

OK, time to give this section the big A and move on to some B words.

bag your head!

back-door bandit

Euphemism for male homosexual.

back door, through the

Achievement via clandestine or underhand means. Side doors are more acceptable.

back o' Bourke

Term used to describe any remote area in the outback of Australia.

back up, to

A little thing we chaps can do to make our wives feel better about their cooking—back up for a second helping. I found a hair in my meatloaf one night. Problem was, it was still growing!

Bags I go next!

A polite way of asking to be next in line or, in the Deputy P.M.'s case, to BE someone!

bags, rough as

Someone or something uncouth and unattractive to the gaze.

Bag your head!

Be quiet, shut-up, get lost . . .

bald as a bandicoot

Well, have you ever sold a wig to a bandicoot?

ball and chain

Generally speaking, your wife. Occasionally, your husband. I've been married to my wife for twenty years. Heck! You only get fifteen for murder!

ball-tearer

Term used to describe something exciting. (See **bollicles**.)

Bananaland

No, not parliament—that's Noddyland. Queensland of course and a native is known as a Bananalander.
(How profound, John!)

bandicoot on a burnt ridge, like a

A bit like me at a disco for under-25s. Alone, forlorn, despairing!

bangs like a dunny door in a gale

The sort of girl a lot of fantasising fellows would like to meet does exactly this—a female frequent fornicator.

like a bandicoot on a burnt ridge

bar, you won't have a . . . of him/her/it

You will have nothing to do with him, her or even it for that matter!

bashing your brains out

The act of thinking or studying very hard. I got through school with grey matter intact!

beak, the

The judge or magistrate. Being a derogatory term, it is not advisable to address the bench as 'Your Beakness'.

bearded clam, spearing the

Fornication. (See **punch in the whiskers**.)

beef bayonet

> The penis. I don't think that needs any further elaboration. Should you wish to find further euphemisms for this appendage, keep reading, mark them with a highlighter—then, call your analyst!

beef to the ankles

beef to the ankles

> Fat. How fat? When he bent over in a restaurant to tie his shoelaces, the head waiter sat a party of eight around him!

bib, keep your . . . on

> Don't get too excited or upset.

bib, stick your . . . in

> Interfere where you're not wanted.

big girl's blouse

> Effeminate male.

Big Island, the

What Tasmanians call Australia—er, sorry, the mainland!

bike, the town

A promiscuous female. We had a girl in my home town called Door Handle, everyone got a turn!

billiard ball, sharp as a

Not very intelligent.

bit, getting a bit

What old Door Handle was getting!

bit, of all right

Attractive, promising—generally used to describe females.

Bliss, Johnny

Rhyming slang for piss (urinate). It's especially bliss if you've been hanging on for a while.

block, do your

Go crazy, get angry. (See *nana, do your*.)

bloke, like a . . . with boils on his arse

If you were suffering from this condition, you'd be pretty bad-tempered too.

blue-arsed fly, running around like a

Running hither and thither and getting nowhere or nothing done. (See *politician*.)

blue swimmer

A ten-dollar note, thus called because its colour resembles that of the blue swimmer crab.

bodgie

bodgie

Fifties and sixties equivalent of English teddy boy. Characteristics include greased-back hair, pointy-toed shoes, white socks, stove-pipe trousers, long sideburns and a penchant for Buddy Holly. Some are still in existence today—but not a protected species.

bog, to go for a

To defecate.

bog in, to

To start eating feverishly. Part of that inspiring line of Grace, 'Two, four, six, eight—bog in, don't wait.' Or, 'Gather, gather 'round the table, fill yer bellies while yer able.' More tea, Vicar?

bollicles

Euphemism for testicles. If something is exciting or particularly pleasing, it is a 'tearer of bollicles'. (See **ball-tearer.**)

bollocky, in the

In the nude. I was arrested for sun-baking naked, but the judge let me off 'cos he couldn't see exhibit A!

bolter

A long-priced racehorse that wins. I only joined Gamblers' Anonymous because they open each day at 10 to 1. (John!)

bombers, brown or grey

Parking officers from various states, thus called for the colour of their uniforms and the way they launch bombing raids on your car (and your wallet!).

in the bollocky

Bondi tram, to shoot through like a

To depart quickly, generally owing money or rent.

boned up the bum

If you have suffered this misfortune, you have just been cheated.

bone, to point the

Aboriginal custom generally resulting in the death of pointee. Term of accusation now commonly used by white population usually without such lethal consequences.

boofhead

Descriptive term for slow thinker with over-sized head.

boomerang, it's a

Don't you loathe people who say this whenever you borrow something from them?

booze bus

boot, in yer

Exclamation of scorn or rejection.

boot, to put the . . . in

To kick someone (either literally or figuratively) when they're down.

booze bus

Mobile police vehicle used for random breath testing. Now common around Australia. When I got tested I asked the cop if he was going to charge me with being over the limit and he said, 'Yes, just as soon as I get the Breathalyser bag down from the tree!'

bore it up 'em, to

To press home the advantage on the sporting field when your opponents don't stand a chance of winning.

Born in a tent, hey! were you?

Statement directed at anyone who leaves a door open on arrival or departure. I told my doctor some days I feel like a wigwam, other days I feel like a tepee. He said, 'I see your problem, you're too tense.' Sorry about that one—let's keep reading huh?

boss cocky

The man in charge. (Rural derivation.)

Bottle-oh!

Cry of the man who would pay for your empty beer bottles. These days, almost obsolete, but I do recall our bottle-oh calling on our family three times a day!

bowyang

String or leather strap tied below knees of bushmen's trousers—allegedly to stop snakes crawling up their legs.

bowyangs

(1) box

Vulgar term for female genitalia.

(2) box

Protective plastic pouch cricketers wear to protect theirs!

bracket

Your backside. As a child, I often copped a boot up the bracket. In fact, I knew my father like the back of his hand!

brain, if he had another . . . it would be lonely

Derisive description of an idiot.

brains, not enough . . . to give him a headache

Same idiot!

Break it down!

Exclamation demanding fair play.

brick

Formerly a ten-pound note (now $20.00), thus called due to its reddish colour.

bride's nightie, to be up and down like a

Descriptive term for anything that fluctuates wildly or an emotional person.

brinny

Small pebble ideal for skimming across water or for just chucking about.

Britt, going for a Jimmy

Rhyming slang for 'shit'. Jimmy Britt was the former world lightweight boxing champion who toured Australia during World War One. You may also go for an Edgar Britt (no relation and non-existent) and indeed, if you are in a bad mood you are said to have the Jimmies or the Edgars . . . moreover, someone else can give you them!

brothel

Apart from the obvious, it's also a word used to describe a dirty, untidy habitat. My room as a child for instance. A word of warning for tourists. Be wary of a building with a sign that says 'Our Lady of Good Hands'. It may not be a church!

it would kill a brown dog

brown dog, it would kill a

Used to describe any food or drink that it is impossible to consume. My wife's cooking is so bad, the airlines ring *her* for recipes!

Bruce

Uttered with lots of sibilance it becomes a euphemism for a male homosexual (with apologies to all the Bruces reading this) and, uttered without sibilance, it becomes a British term for the average Aussie male.

bucket of prawns in the sun, goes off like a

Term used to describe a promiscuous woman. Take out 'goes' and it can also mean to depart hastily.

bucket, tip the . . . on

To expose hitherto unknown facts in order to embarrass the bucketee.

Buckley's chance

No chance whatsoever. Derived from former Melbourne department store, Buckley and Nunn. 'He's got two chances—Buckley's and none!'

bugle, a bang on the

A punch on the nose.

bugle, on the

Smelly or dubious.

Bugs Bunny

Rhyming slang for money. I just wove that wascally wabbit!

bull at a gate, like a

Impatient people tackle tasks in this manner without thought for the consequences.

bull, couldn't hit a . . . in the bum with a handful of wheat

Thank God William Tell never suffered from this problem. Alas, some of our cricketers do!

bum, bite your

Dismissive exclamation of scorn (and physically impossible).

bundle, dropped her

Vulgar expression describing childbirth.

bundle, dropped his

When he found out he was the father he totally lost control of his senses he did (and serves him right!).

Bundy

Abbreviation of Bundaberg rum, manufactured in the Queensland town of same name and the best red rum in the universe. (Please send crates c/o publisher!)

bung, gone

In a state of disrepair, not working, cactus, useless.

(1) bunny

Tail-end batsmen. So-called due to ineptitude with bat (Merv Hughes excepted) and the way they jump around when faced with a fast delivery.

(2) bunny

Someone easily fooled, who cops the blame for something not necessarily of his or her doing.

burglar

A golfer who plays better than his or her handicap in order to win money or respect from opponents. Generally regarded to be low down in the food chain. I'm no burglar—in fact, the last time I played golf, the only two decent balls I hit all day was when I stood on a rake in a bunker. Ow!

(1) Burke and Wills

Rhyming slang for dills. One dill is generally called a Burke.

(2) Burke and Wills, covered more ground than

Often used to describe a horse that races wide, in memory of those trans-continental explorers from the last century.

go for a burn

burn, to go for a

Something you do in a car when you take it out for a quick spin. Don't get caught by the cops or you'll go for a row!

(1) bushed

Totally lost.

(2) bushed

Totally exhausted.

get along like a bushfire

bushfire, to get along like a

To enjoy someone's company. (See also ***house on fire***.)

bushie

See ***bushwhacker***.

bush lawyer

Someone who gives you unqualified (and sometimes unwelcome) legal advice.

(1) bushrangers

Another term for golfers who play better than their handicaps. I'm known as a bushranger but only because I spend so much time in the bushes looking for my ball!

(2) bushrangers

People who charge exorbitant fees. Like my accountants, Grabbit & Run!

bush telegraph

Originating from early days when informants would alert bushrangers of approaching police, its modern day word-of-mouth counterpart is the grapevine.

Bush Week, waddya think it is?

Exclamation of derision or retort aimed at someone transparently trying to dupe you. If successful, the dupor generally replies to the dupee . . .'Yeah, and you're the sap!'

bushwhacker

Someone who hails from a rural area—or who acts like it.

busier than a one-armed paper hanger/taxi driver with the crabs

Sort of self-explanatory really. But if you don't believe me, tie one arm behind your back and try scratching and driving at the same time!

busier than a one-armed taxi driver with
the crabs

but

Used as emphasis at the end of a sentence when conversing. Common to certain States (except Victoria but!).

butter wouldn't melt in his/her mouth

Someone who sounds and looks perfect and angelic but beware . . . that butter is probably rancid!

chewie on your boot

cacked

Something you did in your pants when you laughed too much or when you were terrified. 'He cacked himself laughing.'

camp as a row of tents

Blatantly homosexual—roaring out of the closet at a hundred kilometres per hour.

Centre, the

The middle of Australia where men are men and the sheep are nervous! Sometimes called the Red Centre.

century, to knock up a

To hit a hundred or more runs in a cricket match.

chain, dragging the

Not putting in a full effort or not keeping up with a 'shout' in the pub.

chalkie

A school teacher. I hated my teacher. She failed me at plasticine—it ruined my sixteenth birthday!

charge like a wounded/Mallee bull, to

To charge too much for goods or services.

(1) cheerio

In the Northern Territory and Queensland these are your small frankfurters. (See also **little boys** and **savs**.)

(2) cheerio

A friendly word of farewell.

(3) cheerio

A greeting generally sent to someone over the radio. 'I'd like to send a cheerio to both my listeners!'

cheese, the old

Short for cheese and kisses, rhyming slang for missus. It can also refer to your mother.

Chesty Bonds

Almost generic name for men's singlets derived from 1930s cartoon character used to promote this brand of clothing.

Chewie on yer boot!

A mild curse directed at a footballer in order to put him off his kicking. In my 40-odd years of yelling this, it never worked!

chiack, to

To tease or jeer.

Chinaman, I must have killed a

Expression to explain bad fortune. I think I must have, everything seems to be going 'wong' lately!

dry as a chip

chip, dry as a

Very thirsty or in a state of drought. I remember the last big drought. It was so bad, they had to close down two lanes of the local swimming pool.

(1) chip in, to

To interrupt or stick your bib in.

(2) chip in, to

Contribute money for someone leaving the office or towards a good cause. Most of my former bosses think they're one and the same in my case!

chockers

chockers

Derived from choc-a-block meaning totally full. Hence the airport announcement: 'Sorry Ockers, all our Fokkers are Chockers!'

chocko

Abbreviation of chocolate frog which is rhyming slang for wog.

chocolate teapot, as useful as a

A bit like the ashtray on that motorbike, totally useless.

chooks, I hope your . . . turn into emus and kick your dunny down

Ancient Aussie curse. The problem is, by the time you've finished saying it, the cursee is out of earshot!

chop, get in for your

Grab your fair share of something.

I hope your chooks turn into emus
and kick your dunny down!

chop, not much

Something inferior or unsuitable.

chop, one . . . short of a barbie

Not the full quid.

choppers

Teeth.

chow shop

Chinese take-away restaurant.

Christmas, what else did yer get for

Witty retort to motorist who gives you an unnecessary blast on the horn. (I always open the car door for my wife, but only at sixty kilometres per hour!)

chromies

Chrome wheels.

chrome dome

A bald person. He's not really bald—he's just grown too tall for his hair!

Clayton's

A satisfactory substitute for the real thing. Derived from advertising slogan for the non-alcoholic drink: 'Clayton's, the drink you have when you're not having a drink!'

chrome dome

clocked

Struck, hit. 'He clocked him one.'

club, in the

Not exactly exclusive this one. You're pregnant. When the baby's born, Dad spends most of his time *down* the club.

clucky

Physical phenomenon occurring in women handling someone else's newborn baby. Husbands are advised to book a fishing trip with the boys when this condition manifests itself.

Coathanger, the

The Sydney Harbour Bridge.

coat lifter

A male homosexual.

coat tailer/tugger

Generally found at racecourse tugging at your coat for money or a tip. If he attempts to *lift* your coat, he may not be a punter!

cockatoo

Person who keeps watch for the police at an illegal gambling venue.

(1) cocky

Abbreviation of cockroach (or cockatoo).

(2) cocky

Self confident, arrogant—in fact, up yourself.

cocky's poop, not worth a pinch of

> I've checked with my commodities broker—he tells me I should have put my money in soya beans instead! Anyone wanna buy 50 tonnes of cocky manure?

coit

> Your bum. (See also **quoit**.)

colder than a mother-in-law's kiss

> Extremely cold. Every time mine visits, our central heating starts up.

colder than a mother-in-law's kiss

cold enough to freeze the balls off a billiard table

And if that's not cold enough . . .

cold enough to freeze the walls off a bark humpy

Corruption of 'cold enough to freeze the balls off a brass monkey'.

collected, to get

What happens to you if your opponent runs through you in a football match or you don't look both ways crossing the road. I got collected last week—I didn't get his registration number but I'd know that laugh anywhere!

Collins Street farmer

City dweller who owns a farm but who would not know one end of a sheep from another.

come at, I couldn't . . . that

Total rejection of a proposal or proposition. I *know*, I've had a *lot* of women say it to me.

Come off it!

Expression of cynicism and disbelief.

compo

Abbreviation of compensation benefits. Can you get compo for writer's cramp? No? OK, I'll keep writing!

connie

Abbreviation for tram conductor or conductress. I asked one how, long the next tram would be and she said, 'Oh, about twelve metres!'

Coolgardie safe

Hessian-covered frame which is kept moist to preserve perishable foodstuffs.

cop it, to

To receive punishment, usually verbal. 'You're gunna cop it for getting home so late.'

copping it sweet

So when you do cop it, take your punishment and agree with everything your wife says. It'll drive her crazy!

cop-you-later

Corruption of 'copulator', it means simply, 'see you soon'. Never use this term when bidding farewell to a visiting priest.

cornflakes packet, where did you get your licence, out of a

On-road curse shouted at incompetent motorist who has inconvenienced you. (Other cereals also acceptable.)

crack

Your anus.

crack a fat, to

To have an erection. Remember the famous Arab actor Yasser Crackafat?

crackerjack

Adjective describing anything or anyone outstandingly good.

cracker, you don't have a

You're devoid of funds, you haven't got two sticks to rub together, you're broke, skint, stony broke, haven't got not a brass razoo . . .

doesn't have a cracker

crack hardy, to

To put a brave face in adversity.

cracking on

The act of chatting up another person with the aim of seduction. Cracking on is an acceptable male or female practice. Just don't let your respective spouses catch you at it.

crash hot

Really good, great, fantastic.

cray

Abbreviation of crayfish (lobster).

crook

> Sick.

crook, to go

> To complain or admonish.

cross-country wrestling

> What Aussie Rules fans call Rugby League.

crows, stone the

> Exclamation of surprise.

cruel the pitch, to

> To spoil someone's fun.

crumpet, not worth a

> Totally worthless. That's weird—at our local supermarket, crumpets are around $1.20 a packet.

cue, to put one's . . . on the rack

> You've either died or stopped fornicating or retired—the last is most appealing.

Cupid, my name's . . ., not stupid

> Reassuring comment that you're not easily fooled.

cut lunch, to throw a

> Rhyming slang for throw a punch.

cuts, the

School corporal punishment of receiving several strokes of a leather strap across the palms of the hand. I was just made to stand in the corner. In fact it happened so often, I spent most of my school life thinking I was a fern!

the cuts

death adders in your pocket

daggy

Descriptive term for anything unfashionable or out of date—generally worn by dags.

dags

Unmentionable substances hanging off a sheep's bottom.

daily double

If you achieve two successes, you've got the daily double: the racing term for picking winners of two designated races. An ancient Aussie quip is: 'I've seen better legs on a daily double.'

Dame Nellie, doing a

Retiring, then coming back again and again. Derived from Australian opera singer Dame Nellie Melba (1861–1931) who kept doing just this.

Darwin stubbie

Understated size of Northern Territory two litre bottle of beer.

date

Your anus—no doubt due to the resemblance to this fruit! To this day, I still can't eat them!

dated

If a friend sneaks up behind you and affectionately grabs you between the buttocks, you have just been dated!

dead dingo's donger, drier than a

Pretty damn thirsty.

dead horse

Rhyming slang for tomato sauce. You put it on your dog's eye (pie).

dead horse, flogging a

Indulging in a pointless exercise.

dead set

Absolutely true, fair dinkum, a certainty.

death adders in your pocket

You have a reluctance to pull out your wallet to pay your fair share.

deener

Pre-decimal term for a shilling (now ten cents).

Dick, had the

Variation on 'had the Richard'. Something has outlived its usefulness.

dickless Tracy

A female police officer (for obvious reasons). Frisk me officer, I may have a gun!

diff, what's the

Abbreviation of 'what's the difference?'

dill

Idiotic, stupid person who thinks Fred and Wilma Flintstone are married in real life.

(1) dinger

A condom. I know this because my birth certificate is a letter of apology from the Acme Condom Company.

(2) dinger

Seldom-used term for penis.

(3) dinger

Seldom-used term for anus.

done like a dinner

dinner, done like a

> Thoroughly defeated.

dip

> A pick-pocket. I've got them beaten though. I leave a note in my pocket saying 'Sorry, the Tax Department has just beaten you to it!'

dip, have a

> Get involved in a punch-up.

dip out on, to

> To miss an opportunity or renege on an agreement.

dirty, to be a bit . . . on

> To be angry with someone.

dirty, to do the . . . on

> That's exactly how to make someone a bit dirty on you. To betray a trust.

dishlickers

dishlickers

Greyhounds. (*See also **rats on sticks**.*)

(1) do

A party.

(2) do

A hairdo. A nymphomaniac is any woman who has sex half an hour after having a hairdo!

dog, head like a robber's

Generally used to describe an ugly female. I wouldn't say my first girlfriend was ugly but, she was great at catching frisbees in her mouth!

dog's balls, to stick out like

To be obvious.

Don, the

Sir Donald Bradman, Australia's finest batsman.

dong

The penis.

donger

The penis—roughly same size as a dong!

donkey, why don't you turn into a . . . and get on yourself!

A term used to tell someone to wise-up.

why don't you turn into a donkey and get
on yourself!

do over

> To beat the living daylights out of someone. To knock someone's teeth so far down his throat, he has to stick a toothbrush up his bum to clean them. To hit him so hard he gets picked up for speeding in an adjacent suburb. OK, I think you've got the message on that one.

(1) dose, to cop a

> To contract venereal disease.

(2) dose, to cop a

> To be soundly berated for your incompetency.

dose of salts, go through like a

> Refers to a thorough beating. In a game of football, if your opponent does this to you, it takes you a little while to get up again.

dot

> Your anus.

down under

What youse foreigners call Australia. Then there was the Aussie pop star who went on a tour of America and told all the girls he was very big down under.

dragged, to be

The act of the coach pulling you off (the field, that is) during the game of Aussie Rules football.

draining the dragon

Urinating. (See also **syphon the python**.)

drier than a Pommy's bath towel

drier than a Pommy's bath towel

Uncomplimentary suggestion that our friends from the Old Dart don't wash too often. Personally, I shower at least once a month—whether I need to or not.

drop a bucket

drop a bucket, to

To expose hitherto unknown embarrassing facts about someone.

drum, didn't run a

Turf parlance for a horse that didn't run as well as expected. I know the feeling—I backed a horse the other day at 20-1. It finished the race at 3-30.

drum, to be given the

To be given inside information. Someone gave me the drum this book would be a best-seller—I told him to beat it!

duckhouse, that's one up against your

Expression used whenever you've gained some advantage over your opponent.

duck-shove

To move something around often enough so that ultimately you are not responsible for it. (See also **politician**.)

duck, wet enough to bog a

Very wet. It was so wet in the city last week, I saw two ducks fighting for a taxi.

duffer

A worthless gold mine. Anyone wanna buy my 2000 Duffer Corp. shares?

dummy

What the Yanks call a baby pacifier. My mum used a mallet!

dummy bid

A bid taken at a house auction by a real estate agent to increase the value of the sale. These bids are generally put in by a friend of the vendor, a letter box or a tree. Buyer beware!

wet enough to bog a duck

dummy bid

dummy, spit the

To lose your temper, stack on a tantrum.

durry

A cigarette or cigarette butt. Have you ever noticed people who give up smoking replace it with another annoying habit? Like talking about it.

euchred after getting your end in

early opener

Hotel that opens around 6am to cater for shift workers. I was driving home from one the other morning when a cop pulled me over and said, 'You're drunk, your car was weaving all over the road!' I said, 'Thank God for that, I thought my steering had gone!'

eighteen

An eighteen-gallon keg of beer or, if you only need enough to keep the party going till lunchtime, you can just order a 'niner'!

Ekka, the

The Brisbane Exhibition Grounds. Also distinctly Australian abbreviation of the name Eric.

emu

Chaps who roam around racecourses picking up discarded betting tickets in the hope one will be a winner. They'd starve to death picking up mine!

emu parade

> Military or school parade assembled to clean up litter.

end, getting your . . . in

> Having sexual intercourse.

En-Zed

> Abbreviation for New Zealand. I could tell you that En-Zedders have found two new uses for sheep—wool and meat. But I won't.

euchred

> Worn-out, exhausted, useless—which is how I feel at the moment—and I'm only up to E!

pick the eyes out of

eyes, pick the . . . out of

> To examine in detail. If the literary critics do it to this book, I'm in deep trouble.

fat as a match

Fair crack of the whip!

Exclamation demanding fair play.

Fair suck of the sauce bottle!

Exclamation demanding a fair crack of the whip.

Fair suck of the sav!

Exclamation demanding a fair suck of the sauce bottle.

Fanging it

Driving your car really fast—from the name of Argentinian racing-car driver, Juan Fangio. Last time I got picked up for speeding, the cop said he'd let me off with a warning . . . so he fired a shot over my head!

fat as a match

A build of person who has to run around in the shower to get wet.

Father's Day, happy as a bastard on

As you would imagine, not too happy. I have a feeling I was an unwanted child. My parents used to give me bath toys like toasters and hair dryers!

fattie

Euphemism for $1000.00.

fatties

Wide car tyres.

feather duster, rooster one day, . . . the next

We've had our share of these in Australia over the past few years. A self-explanatory term.

fence, a bit over the

Anything unreasonable. My royalties for instance.

fencing wire, as tough as

You can't get much tougher than that!

ferret, giving the . . . a run

Having sexual intercourse.

fess up, to

To confess.

fibro

Any house made from fibro-cement sheeting. Because this material is relatively cheap, seaside resorts abound with fibro cottages around Australia.

fit as a Mallee bull

Full of strength and vitality. If you're feeling even better than this, you are fit as a Mallee bull, only twice as dangerous!

fiz-gig

Originally a term used to describe a police informer but these days used to describe someone whose name you can't recall. 'You remember old fiz-gig dontcha?'

flat out like a lizard drinking

Working at a feverish pace.

drinking with the flies

flies, drinking with the

Unsociable types who drink alone are indulging in this practice.

flick, to get the

To be either fired from your job or to be rejected. 'Bernie gave his girlfriend the flick last week.'

flies, no . . . on him

Describes someone who is astute and not easily duped. A lot of people say there are no flies on me, but you can see where they've been.

(1) flog

To steal.

(2) flog

To sell (possibly something you've just flogged).

flogger

A large bunch of team-coloured paper streamers attached to a stick and waved frantically whenever your team kicks a goal or to distract the opposing full-forward while he's trying to kick one.

flogging the log

Masturbating.

flying fox

Something you can't catch from the previous activity. Rhyming slang for the pox (venereal disease).

Flynn, in like

To be successful in seducing a woman. Allegedly originating in the sexual prowess of Australian actor, Errol Flynn.

form, how's your rotten

Mild astonishment for someone who's had some good fortune but who didn't include you.

after drinking some fourpenny dark

fourpenny dark

Really cheap red wine. It can double as paint stripper and leaves your mouth tasting like the bottom of a cocky's cage!

franger

Euphemism for condom.

Freddie, Blind

Imaginary person used to accentuate the obvious. 'Even Blind Freddie could see that coming!'

free

A free kick in Aussie Rules footy.

freight

Money.

Fremantle doctor

A cooling afternoon breeze in Fremantle and Perth—thus called because doctors are supposed to make you feel better. My doctor is really strange, he keeps a celebrity specimen collection!

French letter

A condom. A ten-year-old got one out of a machine at the airport and told his mum, 'This is the worst chewing gum I've ever tasted!'

Frenchy

Another condom.

front, front up

Show up somewhere or appear before the court. For example, front the judge or magistrate.

froth, couldn't blow the . . . off a beer

Extreme lack of strength—I think I'll just drink it instead!

fuck truck

A panel van used for stuff you normally do in a sleazy motel room (only cheaper). (See also **shaggin' wagon**.)

full as a goog

Pretty damn drunk or full of food.

fuller than a Catholic state school

Pretty damn drunk!

fuller than a seaside dunny on Boxing
Day

fuller than a seaside dunny on Boxing Day

Very similar condition to the goog and the Catholic state school.

Fuzzy Wuzzy angels

Military jargon for New Guinea natives who acted as stretcher-bearers during World War Two.

gerry

'G', the

Abbreviation for the world's most magnificent sporting stadium—well, I *am* a Melburnian—the Melbourne Cricket Ground (MCG).

Gabba, the

Abbreviation for the world's most magnificent sporting stadium well, I *would* like this book to sell well in Queensland—the Queensland Cricket Association oval. So named as it's situated in the suburb of Woollon-'gabba'.

G and C

Graft and corruption.

galah session

Gossip session on the Royal Flying Doctor radio network. My doctor is really weird—tells me to take off my clothes then goes to the roof of a building across the road with a pair of binoculars!

game as Ned Kelly

Very brave, foolhardy.

game as a pissant

More bravado, possibly brought on by the effects of alcohol.

Geebung

Now a generic name for any remote town or uncultivated native-born Australian and described thus in A B Paterson's poem: 'It was somewhere up the country, in a land of rock and scrub,/that they formed an institution called the Geebung Polo Club.'

A geebung is also a native plum—described as a small and tasteless fruit . . . and I've worked with a few of those in television over the years!

geek, to take a

To take a look at something. You are taking a geek at this book.

gerry

An older person (geriatric). I'm not saying Grandpa is old but, he *has* seen Halley's Comet six times!

get off yourself

Stop boasting about yourself.

ghost, grey

Parking officer (Victoria) where, due to the incidents of assault by irate motorists, they now work in pairs. Thank God for that—for a minute there I thought they were breeding!

gig, take a

Take a look.

gig

Strange, eccentric person who can also be a little stupid.

giggle house

Mental asylum. (See **parliament**.)

ging

Primitive slingshot generally made from a strip of rubber inner tube.

(1) ginger

Your anus.

(2) ginger

Horse manure, so called because of its colour.

Ginger Meggs

Perennially youthful Australian cartoon character constantly having the living daylights belted out of him by the perennially violent Tiger Kelly.

giveaway

Inadvertent admission or clue. This book is a dead giveaway that I was absent from school the day they did English Expression!

give away, to

To abandon or give up on something.

glass door, as useful as a . . . on a dunny

Fairly useless.

as useful as a glass door on a dunny

glory box

A container used by prospective brides to store all their marital aids in: Toasters, hairdryers, clothes, vertical grills, frypans, et cetera. (US—hope chest.)

gnat's nasty, missed by a

Missed by that much, Chief! If you don't know how small a gnat's nasty is, it's a little smaller than a bee's dick.

goat, ran like a hairy

I've backed a few racehorses that have run like this over the years. Still, it always takes about twenty horses to beat mine most times so they can't all be bad!

Godzone

Strine for God's Own Country. Australia of course.

goer

A fast performer—car, horse, woman et cetera. I hope this dictionary is one!

going the knuckles

Fisticuffs.

golly

A pimple. I had so many as a teenager, the rest of the kids used to hold me down and play join-the-dots!

gone for a ride on the padre's bike

Statement to cover someone's whereabouts.

gone to Gowing's

Slogan of Sydney retail store in the 1940s. If a town is deserted, it's assumed the population has 'Gone to Gowing's' for the bargains.

gone for a ride on the padre's bike

Gong

An award. I am a member of the Federation of Australia Radical Talkers' Society but prefer not to have initials after my name!

gong, had the

Tired, useless, cactus!

Gong, the

Abbreviation of New South Wales city of Wollongong.

Good on yer!

Well done!

good, to come

To get better or recover.

(1) go off, to

To indulge in sexual intercourse. If a girl 'goes off', she is generally much sought after.

(2) go off, to

To putrefy.

(3) go off, to

To be stolen.

(1) gooley

A small stone used for throwing.

(2) gooley

An unspeakable thing that hangs out of your nose.

goom

Aboriginal term for methylated spirits. My great uncle died from drinking too much of this stuff—a horrible death but it was a lovely finish!

Gordon, in more trouble than Speed

Comic-strip character always in strife. (US—Flash Gordon.)

gorilla

Euphemism for $1000.00.

grafter

Hard worker.

graft, to

To work hard. Most of us graft out a living (unless we can get on to a bit of the **graft and corruption**).

grand piano, couldn't find a . . . in a one-roomed house

Stupid, inefficient. So stupid, if his IQ was five points lower, he'd be a geranium.

Granny Smiths

Bright green apples named after Maria Ann Smith who died in 1870.

grape on the business, a

A spoilsport.

grass castles

Contemporary term for mansions built on the proceeds of the sale of marijuana. Now, if I give little Johnnie three marijuana cigarettes and he smokes one of them, how many does he *think* he has left?

grass castles

greasy pig

Finally throwing tails after a succession of heads in a game of two-up.

Great White Shark

Australian golfing great, Greg Norman. Me? They call me the Great White Flake!

greenie

An environmentalist. Seen recently, a bumper sticker saying 'Help fertilise the earth—bury a Greenie!'

Gregory Peck

Rhyming slang for cheque (also goose's neck). My bank manager phoned to say my cheque account was overdrawn. I yelled at him. 'Do I call you when you've got too much of *my* money?' My wife's even better. Whenever we're overdrawn, she just writes another cheque to cover it!

grouter, to come in on the

To take unfair advantage of a situation, a bit like taking home a girl your mate's been chatting up all night.

Grout, Wally

Rhyming slang for stout (the drink) or snout. (From Wally Grout—the famous wicket keeper for Australia.)

guernsey, to get a

To win a place in a football team or to be accepted generally.

gum-sucker

A native of Victoria. The 'gum' is for gumleaves—not those things that hold your teeth in!

happy as a possum up a gumtree

gumtree, happy as a possum up a

> Blissfully contented.

gumtree, up a

> Stranded, needing help. Almost the opposite of that bloody possum on the next branch!

gun

> A top-class shearer.

guts, in the

> Right in the middle. A ball kicked through the middle of the goal-posts is said to be through the guts.

guts, rough as

> An unattractive or uncouth person deserves this description.

guts, spilling your

> Confessing all.

gutter gripper

> You see 'em everywhere don't you? Motorists driving along with their arm out the window gripping the roof gutter.

gymp

> Anyone who walks with a limp. That's l-i-m-p (pronounced limp!).

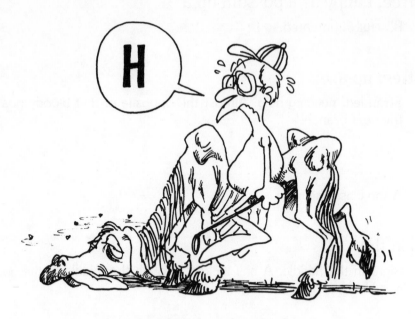

couldn't head a duck

hair, grown too tall for his

Going bald. I've painted little rabbits over my bald patch so from a distance they look like hares. Please keep reading—the gags can't get much worse!

half-back flanker

Rhyming slang for wanker.

hammer, to be on someone's

To pressure someone from behind.

handbag

Male companion (sometimes homosexual) to woman who needs a partner at social function. This subterfuge works well for both parties—everyone thinks he's straight and she can get any man she likes!

happy as Larry

> Bit like the possum up that gumtree.

happy as a pig in muck

> Happy as Larry!

Harbour City, the

> Sydney, of course! Also known as 'Steak and Kidney'.

hard word, putting the . . . on

> Either asking for some sexual recreation or borrowing money.

hatful, ugly as a . . . of arseholes

> You can't get much uglier than that—so ugly, whenever you go to the beach, the tide refuses to come in!

have on, to

> To dupe or deceive.

head a duck, couldn't

> Racing parlance for inferior racehorse.

heading 'em

> Throwing 'heads' in a game of two-up.

head like a twisted sandshoe

> Remarkably ugly!

head, pull your . . . in!

> Be quiet! Shut up! Desist or I'll pull it in for yer! Acceptable retort at a football match.

head, I've seen better . . . on a beer

Yet another way of indicating how unattractive someone is.

scarce as hen's teeth

hen's teeth, scarce as

Very rare. And another thing—how come chickens don't have lips either?

herbs, giving it some

Used to describe the act of accelerating a car.

hide the sausage/weenie

No, not a game played at a tot's birthday party—we are talking fornication here! (See also **sink the sav**.)

hip pocket in a singlet, as useful as a

Yet another in a long line of useless things.

hip-pocket nerve

Located just near your wallet. It tends to ache every time you pay for something. The government knows exactly where to find it.

holding

State of financial liquidity. 'How ya holding? Couldn't lend us a quid could ya?'

hollow log

Rhyming slang for bog (to defecate).

home and hosed

Racing term for horse that wins by such a large margin, it's already in the stable being hosed down while *my* horse is still running.

home with a rug on

Same race—same horse!

homing pigeons, couldn't lead a flock of

Incompetent leader. Space restrictions and the laws of libel prevent me from naming the politicians and former superiors I had in mind!

hooks, to put the . . . into

To borrow money.

hoop

A jockey.

horse, I'm so hungry I could eat a . . . and chase the jockey

Now if you're that hungry, you've got a problem. My fat friend Elmo is the only bloke I know who stands in front of his microwave screaming, 'HURRY'!

horse's hoof

A male homosexual—rhyming slang for poof. Can be shortened to, 'He's a real horse's'.

I'm so hungry I could eat a horse and
chase the jockey

hospital pass

Football parlance for pass given to team-member under imminent pressure. After you catch it and your opponent goes through you, it's straight off to hospital!

hotter than a shearer's armpit

Not that I've ever been that close to a shearer—but very hot.

hottie

Abbreviation for hot water bottle. I woke up this morning and mine had sprung a leak—and I don't even own one.

house on fire, to get on like a

To enjoy someone's company and discover many things in common.

Hughie

Euphemism for the powers that be. Hang on! That's another euphemism isn't it? The gods 'Send her down Hughie!'—an ancient incantation of drought-stricken farmers.

hospital pass

colourful racing identity

icebergs

Men and women who swim in the ocean in the dead of winter. Not for me thanks—it was so cold the other morning, I saw a dog stuck to a tree!

ice drill

Very similar activity to the above except that you are forced to participate by a sadist. Early morning physical exercises conducted in shorts only.

ice-o

Distant relation to the bottle-oh and the rabbit-oh. The man who used to bring the ice of course!

identity, colourful racing

Euphemism for racetrack patron of dubious character.

illywhacker

Confidence trickster operating around country shows.

I'm-all-right-Jackness

Indifference to the welfare of others.

improve, on the

If someone's been ill and is getting better, they are said to be on the improve.

iron lung, wouldn't work in an

Lazy, indolent.

Ities:

(Pron: Eye-tyes.) Abbreviation for Italians. Originated during World War Two.

salute the judge

jack/jacksie

Buttocks, anus.

(1) Jack and Jill

The (contraceptive) pill. Jack and Jill went up the hill to fetch a pail of water. Silly Jill forgot her pill and now they've got a daughter. Pathetic isn't it?

(2) Jack and Jill

Never call for this at a restaurant unless you've got the money to pay. Rhyming slang for the bill.

jack, got the

You now have a venereal disease—do not pass 'Go', do not collect $200.00, go straight to the clinic!

jack, to get . . . of

To become fed up with someone or something. My wife got jack of me years ago—but she says I'm better than nothing. She's such a romantic!

jack up, to

To refuse to do something.

jake, she'll be

Everything will be all right, all right?

Jessie, more hide than

Outrageous, outlandish and bold. (Jessie was the name of a popular elephant at Sydney Zoo in the early 1930s.)

judge, to salute the

What a racehorse does when it wins. How *do* horses salute without falling over?

jumper, stick it up your

Exclamation of rejection. You can also stick it up another fundamental orifice. What's the difference between Telecom and a pelican? Nothing— they can both stick their bills up their bum.

jump, take a running . . . at yourself

Get lost, scram, beat it!

junket trumpet

The penis. Classy!

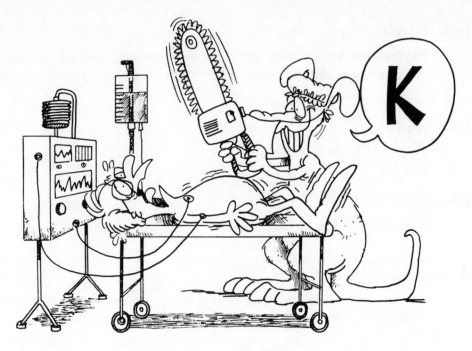

go under the knife

kangaroo hopping

Making your car lurch forward by taking your foot off the clutch suddenly. Generally achieved by learner drivers. It took my first girlfriend twenty attempts to get her licence, just couldn't get used to that front seat!

kangaroos, to keep . . . in the top paddock

A bit stupid. Kangaroos are regarded as vermin by a lot of graziers you see.

kick a goal, to

To achieve a measure of success or persuade a member of the opposite sex to have intercourse with you (and we're not talking the verbal variety here).

kick in, to

To contribute money for a good cause. It's also called 'kicking the tin' as opposed to 'kicking the bucket' in which case friends would 'kick in' for the deceased's family. Got that? Good, let's move on to the next word then.

(1) kick on, to

To achieve financial success.

(2) kick on, to

To go from one social function or pub to another with the express purpose of increasing one's enjoyment.

kick, wouldn't get a . . . in a stampede

Term used to describe an out-of-form footballer. Some teams are so bad, they do a victory lap if they just win the toss!

kindy

Abbreviation of kindergarten. Boy, was my kindy tough! The school bus used to just slow down to let me off!

king hit

A surprise punch generally delivered from behind.

knife, to go under the

To be operated on. My surgeon's really sadistic. First he hands you his bill, *then* he takes your blood pressure!

knock

Sexual intercourse.

knockback

A refusal.

knock back, to

Something you do with a beer—especially if you've just copped a knockback from the girl with the big knockers you've just been given a knockdown to!

knockdown

An introduction to a member of the opposite sex.

knocker, on the

Spot on, precisely, exactly!

(1) knockers

Breasts (aka **norks**).

(2) knockers

People who constantly find fault or deride others' success.

knock shop

A brothel. My great-uncle George went broke after opening Australia's first do-it-yourself massage parlour.

a kick up the Khyber

Khyber, a kick up the

You've just been booted up the backside. Khyber: abbreviation of Khyber Pass (rhyming slang for arse).

Khyber, to be given the

You've either just been fired or someone has rejected you.

lollyboy

Larry Dooley, to give someone

To administer a thorough tongue-lashing or sound thrashing.

lash, to give it a

To make an attempt, have a go at something.

last shower, I didn't come down in the

I'm not as stupid as you think I am!

leg opener

Vulgar expression for use of alcohol pertaining to women. Sorry girls, I'm just the writer!

lemon and sarse

Very similar expression to Khyber Pass. It rhymes with the same part of the anatomy. Sarse: abbreviation of sarsaparilla, a cola-like soft drink.

lezzo

Uncomplimentary term for lesbian. Question: At a lesbian wedding, the father of which bride pays for the ceremony?

lid, I dips me

I doff my hat to you.

life, go for your

Decamp very quickly, or could be an invitation to go right ahead!

little boys

Small saveloys. Do I have to draw a picture?

liver, shit on the

In a very bad mood. (See also **muck on the pluck**.)

lizards, starve the

Rural term of disbelief or astonishment.

lollyboy

Young lad selling confectionery and drinks at a cinema or a sporting venue.

lollywater

Any weak, insipid soft drink.

London to a brick

A fictitious wager placed on a certainty. The phrase was popularised by Sydney racecaller Ken Howard (d. 1976). (A brick was a ten-pound note.)

Loo, the

We're talking about an abbreviation for the Sydney suburb of Woolloomooloo—which is *not* pidgin for 'there's a sheep in my dunny'!

lousy bastard

Anyone deemed to be stingy, mean or niggardly deserves this title.

lousy, feeling

Not feeling very well at all.

lower than a snake's belly/arse

Describes a person of low morals or ethics who would sell his or her grandmother. Even lower is anyone who could free-fall from the same orifice.

lumbered, to get

To be caught in the act or to be arrested.

lunch

lumbered, to get . . . with

When no other family member will have your maiden aunt from England as a house-guest and she finishes up staying with you—you have just been lumbered with her. Be nice, she may be worth a fortune!

lunch

Collective euphemism for that part of the male anatomy consisting of penis and testicles. (Refer male ballet dancers.)

lurk, on to a good

If you're receiving benefits for little or no work, you are said to be on a good lurk. (See **politician**.)

dead as a maggot

mad as a cut snake

Either very cross or totally reckless.

mad as a meat axe

Totally bonkers, nuts, crazy . . .

mad he went . . . and they shot him

Facetious phrase to divert searchers from discovering the whereabouts
of a person.

madwoman's breakfast, all over the place like a

Totally confused, untidy or lacking direction. A bit like this book really.

maggot, dead as a

Completely dead, deceased, cactus, had the gong!

mail, the

Inside advice on form heard mainly around racecourses.

mainlanders

What Tasmanians call inhabitants of the mainland of Australia (the Big Island).

mallee root

Rhyming slang for prostitute. (Mallee roots—large roots of various eucalypts.)

mallee root, face like a

No reflection on our working girls but that's a fairly ugly face. In the interests of equality, this description is genderless.

map, to throw a

To be sick. I don't remember eating Bulgaria!

mappa

Now this is complicated. Mappa is short for map of Tasmania, which, being triangular in shape, resembles the female pubic area. I can't be more delicate than that!

marble, to pass in your

To expire, die, cease . . .

mark, to take a

Aussie Rules term meaning to catch the football. Other terms include 'take a screamer', 'go up for a specky' (spectacular) or 'go the big grab'.

matinee session

Sexual activity during lunchtime or afternoon. Personally, I'd rather watch 'Days of Our Lives'.

matinee session

mean, so . . . that

He wouldn't give you the time of day.
He wouldn't piss on you if you were on fire.
He wouldn't shout if a shark bit him.
He wouldn't give a dog a drink at his mirage.
He wouldn't give a rat a railway pie.
He wouldn't give you a wave if he owned the ocean.
He wouldn't give you the wind off his fart.   And that's pretty mean!

Mediterranean back

Dubious back injury declared in order to claim worker's compensation. So called as it allegedly is more prevalent amongst migrant groups.

merchant

There are various categories for these: standover, panic, king-hit et cetera. They are all specialists in their own particular field.

merchant banker

Rhyming slang for wanker.

metho addict

Person addicted to methylated spirits. Be careful lighting cigarettes for them!

Mexicans

Victorians—thus called because they live South of the Border.

Mickey, taking the . . . (or Michelle) out of

Taking a rise out of someone in a sarcastic manner.

middy

A 7 oz (200 ml) glass of beer in Western Australia. A 10 oz (300 ml) glass in New South Wales.
  Just to the top thanks!

milker, busier than a one-armed . . . on a dairy farm

Hectic. We don't know what happened to the milker's udder arm! (You may groan here!)

milko

The bloke who delivers the milk of course. Dad always thought I bore a remarkable resemblance to ours!

million, gone a

You're totally defeated with no chance of recovery.

miserable bastard

Miserly niggard or someone who complains incessantly.

monty

A sure thing. 'That horse is a monty to win this race.'

more front than Myer

Bold, brazen, unabashed. The Myer Emporium is the largest department store in the southern hemisphere situated in Melbourne with, as you would imagine, very large street frontage.

Moreton Bay

A wig. Rhyming slang, from Moreton Bay Fig.

morning glory

Waking up with an erection. That's why I hate daylight saving—now I get mine at the bus stop!

motza/motser

A large amount of money.

mousetraps, to have . . . in your pockets

A reluctance to pay your restaurant bill. I told my waiter my steak was bad—so he picked it up and spanked it!

mouth like a horse collar

Your mouth is so big, you could eat an apple through a picket fence.

muck on the pluck

In a foul mood. (Variation on **shit on the liver**.)

muddie

Queensland mud crab—great eating!

to have mousetraps in your pockets

mudguts

Affectionate male greeting for someone whose name escapes you. 'G'day, mudguts!' It is suggested you do not use this form of address when meeting a dignitary.

mudlark/mudrunner

A racehorse that runs well on a wet track.

mullet, like a stunned

In a confused, addled condition.

Murray, on the

Rhyming slang for betting on credit—on the Murray cod (nod).

muss, ball of

Feeling very fit, a ball of muscle in fact!

My oath!

Exclamation of affirmation.

My word!

Same as above.

myxo

Abbreviation of myxomatosis—a disease introduced into Australia's rabbit population to eradicate them (and I suspect into my wife's cooking to eradicate me!).

NAGA award

NAGA award

Awarded to hopeless golfers. An acronym for Not A Golfer's Arsehole. I have Australia's biggest collection! (A naga is also an Aboriginal waistcloth.)

nana, to do your

It's what happens when you lose your temper—you do your nana! (Pronounced nar-nar.)

(1) nark

A spoilsport.

(2) nark, to

To annoy, pester, needle.

nasho

A National Serviceman.

naughty

Euphemism for sexual intercourse. (Also, for the *really* broad-minded—Mr Naughties!)

neck, to go under your

To get in first and gain advantage.

necking it

Drinking straight from the bottle.

Ned Kelly

Anyone who indulges in dubious, dastardly dealings.

neddies, the

Horse racing.

(1) nicked, get

A slightly less aggressive way of telling someone to get stuffed.

(2) nicked, get

You're caught doing something wrong. If this happens, do not tell the arresting officer to get nicked!

nit, to keep

To keep watch at an illegal activity, in order not to get nicked.

no beg pardons

Going full bore at something without any apologies for your zeal.

norks

Breasts (see also, **knockers**.)

norms

Lazy, pot-bellied, idle fellows who never exercise. (From 'Life Be In It' advertising campaign.) Norm is so fat, his tailor told him he couldn't alter his trousers—but he could install landing lights!

Northern Territory champagne

Methylated spirits mixed with health salts. Not only a cheap brew but it certainly gives you a good run for your money.

nose, on the

Anything with a vile smell is said to be on the nose. This also applies to a dubious business proposition.

nude nut

A bald person. Actually, I'm not bald—I'm just experimenting with a 15 centimetre parting.

nuddy, in the

Naked. The last time I visited a nudist colony I saw the most popular bloke there carrying two cups of coffee and six doughnuts—at the same time.

in the nuddy

living off the smell of an oily rag

off like a bride's nightie, to be

If you recall your wedding night, that's pretty quick.

oil, the good

The right (inside) information.

oily rag, living off the smell of an

In poverty-stricken circumstances. We were so poor, if we smelt meat cooking, we knew it was just the cat on fire.

old boiler

Not only an old chook but an uncomplimentary description of a woman approaching middle-age! I say 'uncomplimentary' in deference to any old chooks who may be reading this!

old boy, the

The penis. What's old and wrinkled and hangs out your underpants? Your grandma! Oh, how very witty John.

old fellow, the

Yep! he's raised his ugly head yet again!

old girl, the

Your wife or your mum.

old man, the

Your husband, your father or your old boy!

one-eyed trouser snake

See **old boy, old fellow, old man**! The lengths some people will go to not say that word!

one brick short of a load

Mentally deficient . . . you, know, one grape short of a bunch!

Onkaparinka

Brand name of well-known blankets and rhyming slang for 'finger'.

orchestras

Rhyming slang for testicles. (Orchestra stalls—balls.)

Oscar

Rhyming slang for cash. Oscar Asche was an Australian actor who died in 1936.

outer, on the

Being excluded or not allowed in. At a football or cricket match, if you're not a member, you watch from the outer ground. The worst thing about that is when they run 'outer' grog!

piano player in a brothel

Pacific peso

Contemporary term for the devalued Australian dollar. It's so bad at the moment, our local bank got robbed of $50 000. It had a street value of $3.40.

packing it

Terrified. Derived from World War Two slang term 'packing death', which has something to do with trying not to leave a deposit in your underpants when faced with imminent obliteration.

Paddo

Abbreviation for Paddington, a trendy inner-Sydney suburb. It's so trendy, the local service station has an air-pump in case your Perrier goes flat!

parliament

See also: ***Giggle House, Reps, House of, Yack, all . . . and no yakker, rathouse***.

packing it

paper bag, couldn't fight his way out of a

What a wimp!

pelican shit, a long streak of

Affectionate (?) term for tall, thin, rakish fellow.

persuader, the

A jockey's whip. Come to think of it, you could still see the whip marks on the last piece of meat I ate.

physio

Abbreviation of physiotherapist. Well, when was the last time you heard a rugby player string *six* syllables together?

piano player in a brothel, he's just the

Used to describe someone who is oblivious to what's going on around him. Wonder if he could play 'Quando Quando' while I'm waiting!

Pigs!

An exclamation of disparagement or disbelief. Longer versions include: Pig's Bum! Pig's Arse! or, In a Pig's eye!

pineapple, to cop the rough end of the

To be treated unfairly. Do not attempt this at home without proper training!

pissing in someone's pocket

Sycophancy. For example, 'I think, by buying this dictionary, you are showing exquisite literary taste and manifesting an intellect way above that of mere mortals.'

piss

Euphemism for alcohol.

piss up

A drinking session or party.

piss up, couldn't organise a . . . in a brewery

Obviously someone who is not a good organiser.

Pitt Street farmer

The New South Wales counterpart of Victoria's Collins Street farmer. Both wonder how dairy farmers get the cows to sit on those little milk bottles!

plate, bring a

> A quaint custom of bringing a plate of sandwiches or cakes to a social function to ease the cost of catering.

poke a stick at, more than you can

> Used to express abundance or over-supply. (See *politician*.)

poke in the eye with a burnt stick, better than a

> An expression of consolation for someone who doesn't get exactly what they wanted, but gets something anyway. I hear my wife using this expression a lot—especially when talking to our marriage counsellor!

colder than a polar bear's bum

polar bear's bum, colder than a

I would imagine pretty chilly. The guy who took the bear's temperature should be out of intensive care next week!

pole, up the

Confused, illogical.

pole, wouldn't touch it with a forty-foot

Something dubious. Keep well away.

politician

See also, ***blue-arsed fly, running around like a; duck shove; lurk, onto a; poke a stick at, more than you can.***

(1) pony

A very small glass of beer (about half a normal glass).

(2) pony

In the old currency, 25 pounds.

poo, in the

In trouble.

poor, so . . . he's licking the paint off the fence

Not only that, he's eating the undercoat as well!

porcelain bus, driving the

The act of being on one's knees in front of the toilet, grasping it like a steering wheel and chucking (ancient Australian ritual following **piss up**).

possum, stirring the

Mentioning the unmentionable in order to cause trouble. These days, this expression is shortened to 'stirring'.

pot

In Victoria and Queensland, a large (300 ml) glass of beer. If you drink enough of these, you finish up with a beer pot or pot belly—yes, your feet are still there!

potted, to get

Vulgar term for becoming pregnant. My mum screamed a lot when she had me—and that was just during conception!

pox doctor's clerk, dressed up like a

Anyone who dresses in cheap, gaudy clothes. 'Hey, nice suit, somewhere there's a naked clown walking about!' is a variation on the theme.

prick and ribs, all . . . like a drover's dog

Sinewy, lean and ready for action. I'm more like a drover's corgi!

proppy

To walk with hesitant gait due to minor injury. Generally used in football parlance.

proverbial, up the

Polite way of saying 'Up shit creek without a paddle'—meaning to be in dire straits.

pudding club, in the

You're pregnant again? Haven't you got a television?

pup, the night's a

>It's only early.

(1) put in, to

>To do your fair share of the work.

(2) put in, to

>To inform on or dob in.

to cop a quilting

quack, the

The doctor. Which reminds me, my doctor asked me to go over to his window and stick my tongue out. When I asked why, he said, 'I don't like the guy across the road!'

Queer Street, in

Totally bereft of funds, broke, skint, not a brass razoo . . .

quid, not the full

Mentally deficient or, about 18/6 in the pound or, in today's money, 90 cents in the dollar. The light's on but nobody's home; if he had another brain it'd be lonely, et cetera.

quilting, to cop a

To receive a thorough thrashing. I sold my car to a motorcycle gang. Nice guys—they gave me $10.00 and a quilting!

quince, getting on your

> Someone is making you very irate.

Quist

> See **Adrians**—that's if you haven't had too many!

quoit/coit

> Not only those little rope things you chuck around the deck of the QE II butt (*sic*) something you sit on. Buttocks to you!

about to cop a rabbit-killer for shouting
'rabbit-oh!'

rabbit-killer

Karate-type blow to the back of the neck. Used for quickly killing wounded
rabbits (or, if female, in bed to resist amorous advances by your husband).

rabbit-oh

Bloke who used to wander the streets selling rabbits and yelling, 'Rabbit-
oh!' Yet another quaint Aussie tradition that was 'Hare today, gone
tomorrow.' It's OK, not too many more pages to go!

racehorse

A very thin roll-your-own cigarette.

race off, to

The act of quickly convincing a member of the opposite sex that you
should decamp to your abode immediately for the purposes of carnal
pleasures. Enjoy!

raining, if it was . . . pea soup, he'd only have a fork or . . . tits, he'd come up sucking his thumb

Both expressions of misfortune.

rap, a big

To give someone or something this, is to bestow high praise. I just hope I get a big rap for this book! Any effusive compliments gratefully accepted!

rash, all over him like a

Fawning, touching, feeling, caressing—are you listening Julia Roberts? (Common 43-year-old male fantasy!)

rat, cunning as a shithouse

Extremely shrewd. A person not to be trusted.

rathouse

A lunatic asylum. (I was going to write 'see also **parliament**' but I think by now they're probably considering a class-action suit against me. C'mon fellas, only gaggin'!)

rat, like a . . . up a drainpipe

Opportunistic, quick.

rat, like a . . . with a gold tooth

Insincere.

rats on sticks

Euphemism for greyhounds. (Hardly ever used by their owners!)

raw prawn, don't come the

A distinctly Aussie retort to anyone trying to delude, deceive or hoodwink you with a far-fetched, absurd idea or scheme. You see, us Aussies didn't come down in the last shower, mate.

RBT

Initials for random breath testing. You know you've had too much to drink if you go up to an RBT van and ask for two doughnuts and a cup of coffee!

getting off at Redfern

Redfern, getting off at

Coitus interruptus. Redfern is just before Central Station in Sydney you see. Unfortunately, I got off about ten stations back—I was alone at the time!

red-hot

Beyond reason, overpriced, extreme.

repat, the

Any repatriation hospital.

Reps, House of

Lower House of Federal Parliament (House of Representatives). Personally, I don't think we should be too critical of our politicians. After all, they've done nothing!

rev head

Close relation of a petrol head. Young (and old) people who like to drive fast.

revolving door, couldn't go two rounds with a

Jeff Fenech certainly doesn't fit into this category!

Rice, a roll Jack . . . couldn't jump over

A rather large wad of money. Jack Rice was the name of a champion hurdler (the equine variety).

rice, couldn't knock the skin off a . . . pudding

Close friend of the guy in the revolving door. Very weak!

ring

The anus.

ring wobbler

Sorry, nothing to do with previous word! It's any racehorse that causes wild fluctuations in the betting ring.

roaring-up, to cop a

To receive a severe berating.

rockinghorse poop, as rare as

As you imagine, a very scarce commodity.

as rare as rockinghorse poop

ron, keep one for

Whenever you bot a cigarette, it's quite acceptable to bot another for 'later on'. Get it? 'ron!

rotten, to get

To get drunk.

roughie

A long-odds racehorse—often from the bush.

rug-rat

A small child or baby.

Rules

Abbreviation for Australian Rules football.

a sandwich short of a picnic

saloon passage, to get a

Racing term for horse winning without being impeded by others in the race. Perhaps derived from early nautical expression when the rich would book a 'saloon passage' on a passenger ship.

sandwich, a . . . short of a picnic

Like the bloke who keeps kangaroos in his top paddock—mentally deficient.

sausage, not worth a

Useless.

sav

Abbreviation of saveloy (savoury sausage). (See also **little boys**.)

sav, fair suck of the

Exclamation demanding fair play. See also **Fair suck of the sauce bottle! Fair suck of the sausage!**

saver, have a

To hedge one's bets.

schooner

In New South Wales a 15 oz (425 ml) glass of beer. In South Australia, it's 9 oz (255 ml).

scoot, on the

A drinking spree. You know you've had too much to drink if your breath sets fire to your pillow!

scoot, to

To depart in haste.

scorpions, to have . . . in your pockets

A reluctance to pay your way. Real misers keep mousetraps in there as well! (Along with the death-adders!)

scream blue murder, to

To complain loud and long.

(1) scunge

An untidy, unclean, unkempt person of low morals.

(2) scunge, to

To borrow anything from a cigarette to money or a lawn-mower.

scungies

Very brief male swimming costume. Whenever I wear mine, I *look* scungie!

seen more pricks than a second hand dartboard

As you would imagine—a promiscuous woman.

septic

Rhyming slang for Yank—septic tank.

settler's clock

The kookaburra. So called because it laughs just before dark.

two shaggin' wagons

shaggin' wagon

Panel van used for the purposes of copulation. Fast becoming obsolete due to diminishing number of drive-ins! Last time I went to the drive-in, after going for some icecream and Coke it took me three hours to find out whose car my girlfriend was in!

shake hands with the wife's best friend, to

> To urinate. (We blokes are pathetic, aren't we?)

she'll be right

> Expression of reassurance. (See also **she'll be Jake**.)

shickered

> Drunk.

shingle short, a

> Yet another state of mental deficiency.

shiralee

> Name for a swag (rolled-up blanket containing a swaggie's worldly possessions).

shit creek, up . . . without a paddle

> In a desperate situation.

shit-hot

> High quality or an expert at something.

shoot through, to

> To depart hastily without leaving a forwarding address—which is a shame 'cos the little fella has your hair and your nose!

shot, that's the

> Exclamation of approval.

shot, to take a . . . at

> To pass an inflammatory or critical remark.

shouse

Abbreviation of shit-house (inferior) or indeed, the outside lavatory!

shrapnel

Loose change.

shut the gate

Phrase used to indicate an overwhelming victory.

sick canary, couldn't knock the dags off a

Describes a very weak person.

silly as a two-bob watch

Dopey, stupid, idiotic!

silly as a wheel

Dopey, stupid, idiotic.

sink the sausage, to

To copulate.

sink the sav, to

To sink the sausage.

six o'clock swill

Now abolished in all states, it was the mad, final rush for drinks before pubs closed at six o'clock. These days, it's a 24-hour swill!

six of the best

Six strokes of a leather strap as corporal punishment at school. I had a strange head-master, he gave me six of the best one day, then said, 'Now, do it to me!'

skerrick

Denotes little or nothing. For example, there wasn't a skerrick of food in the fridge.

skinner

The sort of horse bookies love. A long-priced winner, reducing their payout and thus 'skinning' the long-suffering punter.

(1) slag, to

To expectorate. My mate Luigi saw a sign at his local railway station that said 'SPIT ON PLATFORM—FINE $20' He said, 'I spit on platform. I find no $20.00! Oh Gawd! They're getting worse!

(2) slag, to

To slag something or someone is to make derogatory remarks or find fault.

slather, open

A no-holds-barred, free-for-all. A bit like when the boss opens the boardroom bar for all the staff!

sledging

In cricket, making insulting remarks to the opposition like: 'Does your husband play too?' 'Your mother's a camel!' 'Your bra strap's showing!' (And that's the *really* bad stuff!)

sling, copping a

Receiving a bribe or secret bonus.

sledging

sling off at, to

To make scornful, hurtful remarks.

slug, to

To overcharge.

smaller, the . . . the property, the wider the brim

A ruse to convince others you are more affluent than you really are—
like driving a Mercedes when you only have a Volkswagen income.

snakey

In a foul mood.

snatch

Female genitalia.

snip, to

> To borrow money from someone without giving them a chance to refuse.

went for a crap and the sniper got him

sniper, went for a crap and the . . . got him

> An army expression to cover up somebody's whereabouts.

snowing down south, it's

> Your petticoat's showing! 'Thanks John.' 'That's OK Alistair!'

soap, wouldn't know him from a bar of

> You have no idea who this person is. Totally unrecognisable.

so hungry, I could eat the crutch out of a low flying duck

> Or for that matter, the crutch out of a camel driver through a cane chair—ravenous!

SOL

> Polite way of saying 'shit on the liver' if you're not into profanity.

sook

> A cry-baby or wimp. Generally used to describe children.

sort, a good

> An attractive woman (or bloke for that matter!)

soul-case, work the . . . out of

> Work extremely hard for very little money—almost akin to slavery (aka housework).

Speedos

> Brand name that is now almost generic for men and women's swimming costume. By the way, I've overcome being humiliated on the beach. Whenever I see the bully approaching, I kick sand in my own face. Thank you, Charles Atlas!

spider

> A soft drink with a dob of icecream added to the top—delicious!

(1) spinner, come in

> Call to the person tossing the coins in a two-up ring once all bets are laid and the ring is clear.

(2) spinner, come in

> An expression of derision used whenever you've successfully duped some lame-brain.

spit, go the big, to

> To throw up.

splash the boots, to

> To urinate.

sprog

Semen.

spruiker

Loud-voiced person standing outside sideshows or department stores inviting passers-by to sample the wares within.

(1) **s**tack on a turn, to

To throw a tantrum or cause a commotion.

(2) **s**tack on a turn, to

To throw a party. If you don't get invited, you're within your rights to 'stack on a turn'—confusing ain't it?

Starve the lizards!

An exclamation of disbelief.

sticker licker

sticker licker

A South Australian parking officer. All right, who put Super-Glue on this one?

stiff, to be

Suffering misfortune. As they say, you don't have to be dead to be stiff!

stiffy

An erection.

Stone the crows!

Exclamation of disbelief or exasperation.

stonkered

Exhausted, worn-out, very tired.

strike a light!

Exclamation of surprise and/or disbelief.

strike me pink!

Yet anothery just like the othery!

stubbies

Now almost generic. Brand name for men's shorts. Favoured by building workers and holidaying dads!

(1) stuck, get . . . into

This either can mean to tackle a task with great enthusiasm or . . .

(2) stuck, get . . . into

To verbally or physically assault someone. In other words, your wife can get stuck into you for not getting stuck into mowing the lawns!

stuck pig, to squeal like a

To complain bitterly or whinge.

subbie

Abbreviation for sub-contractor. Usually found around building sites—when they show up!

suds

Beer.

sunbeam

I love these! Any piece of crockery or cutlery that doesn't need washing up after a meal. My wife and I fought like hell over our dishwasher. She wanted a General Electric—I wanted a Swedish blonde!

sundowner

Swaggie who arrives at a homestead at sundown—too late to do any work, but just in time for grub. This ploy can work very well in the city too!

sunnies

Sunglasses.

swallowing the anchor

super

> Abbreviation of superannuation. My grandfather invested his in a chicken farm with 20 000 hens and a gay rooster!

swallow the anchor, to

> When a sailor finally settles on shore. My great-uncle Horatio has done just that—even though he had an inflatable girl in every port!

swifty, pull a, to

> To dupe someone.

syphon the python, to

> To urinate.

tart-plate

tack, flat as a

Depressed or despondent.

tack, flat

Very fast.

talent, checking out the

A pastime of both sexes in the never-ending search for the perfect partner. This activity can be conducted in pubs, clubs, plazas, the beach—just about anywhere!

talk, she could . . . under wet cement

Let's not be sexist here. I'm sure there are plenty of blokes capable of never being able to put a sock in it as well!

Tallarook, things are crook in

Phrase used to confirm bad situations. Other expressions include: 'Things are crook at Muswellbrook; 'Things are weak at Julia Creek'; 'Got the arse at Bulli Pass'; 'There's no lucre in Echuca'—but, here's the good news!

'The girls are bandy in Urandangie'!

tan-track merchant.

A male homosexual.

tarp

Abbreviation for tarpaulin.

tart-plate

Sorry girls, here we go again. It's the pillion seat on a motor-bike—assuming any of these male chauvinist biking pigs ever get to meet a decent lady!

taxidermist, go see a

Get stuffed!

tearer of bollicles

Derived from *ball-tearer*, it means something exciting or extremely pleasing.

technicolour yawn

To throw up. I don't imagine you want me to go into detail on this one!

that'll be the day

Not only a great Buddy Holly hit but an exclamation of doubt that something will happen.

threepence, able to turn on

Used to describe a car with a tight turning circle or a player who can change direction with ease. For you youngsters who don't know what a threepence is, these days it's worth about three cents. Hang on, better make that *one*!

throw a leg

Male term for sexual intercourse.

thumbs, a handful of

Very clumsy.

tiger for punishment

Anyone who gives it all in work or sport with no thought to injury.

Tijuana Brass, to be given the

To be fired. Tijuana Brass—rhyming slang for arse. Can be shortened to 'Been given the Tijuana!'

tin-arse

A very lucky person who seems to be constantly winning.

tin tack

Rhyming slang for sack (to be fired) or your back.

tits on a bull, as useful as

Useless.

toe, a bit of

If your car's got this, it has heaps of power. In fact, it would probably suck the doors off that Valiant beside you!

as useful as tits on a bull

toss, arguing the

Pointless debate about inconsequential matters when the argument's been resolved.

towie

Tow-truck operator. My doctor is now a member of the NRMA which means if I get ill within five kilometres of his surgery—he gets me towed in!

town, go to

Can either mean get really angry or an expression of assent. Naked man outside City Hall—policeman asks what he's doing there. He replies, 'Well officer, it's like this. My wife and I were preparing to make love and, after we both got undressed, she said OK Harry, got to town—and here I am!'

tracking square

Going steady (US—dating).

train, couldn't . . . a choko vine over a country dunny

> Incompetent. A choko is probably one of nature's most prolific (and boring) vegetables—next to parsnips, cabbages and my brother-in-law!

tram, on the wrong

> Following an erroneous, mistaken path.

tram, wouldn't know a . . . was up him 'til the conductor rang the bell

> Vague. He wouldn't know his arse was on fire until the fireman put the ladder up!

trap for young players

> A situation novices find themselves in through naivety or inexperience.

go around the traps

traps, to go around the

> The act of checking regular sources of information. Derived from rabbit hunters checking their traps for dead bunnies.

tray

Pre-decimal term for threepence.

trick, can't take a

Never has any luck.

trifecta

Racing term used generally to indicate a succession of three. For example, he got the trifecta—she's rich, beautiful and owns a pub! It can work the other way—his wife left him, his house burnt down and his tax bill just came in!

trimmer, you little

Exclamation of pleasure.

triss

An *effete* male (also homosexual).

trot

You can have either a rough or good one of these. It means a run of bad or good luck respectively.

trots

Either harness racing or the effects of a cocktail of sake and prune juice known as the Oriental Express!

tube, to suck on a

To drink beer direct from a can.

tummy banana

The penis (aka tummy sausage).

trots

tweeds

Trousers or panties.

two bob each way, to have

To vacillate or sit on the fence (two bob—pre-decimal equivalent of twenty cents).

ugly as a hatful

ugly as a hatful

   (Of arseholes.) Not that anyone's ever seen this sight, but I imagine it wouldn't be pretty!

ump

   Abbreviation for umpire (especially in Victoria and Australian Rules states. Rugby states call them refs—referees).

underground mutton

   Rabbit.

up a gum tree

   Stranded.

up a wattle

   Either in dire straights or totally mistaken.

uphill, pushing shit . . . with a sharp stick

> As you would imagine, a very difficult task!

Up the mighty . . .!

> Insert name of your favourite footy team: Lions, Pies, Crows, Roosters, Dons, Doggies, Cats, Saints, Blues, Eagles, Bears, Tigers, and any others I may have forgotten.

up who, who's . . . and who's not paying the rent?

> World War Two slang used to establish just who is in charge.

Up yours for the rent!

> Dismissive exclamation which essentially means 'get stuffed!'

there's a light on the verandah but
nobody's home

Vandemonian

Obsolete term for Tasmanian. Derived from that state's original name—
Van Diemen's Land.

Vaseline Valley

Vulgar term for the gay area of Oxford Street, Sydney. I know a married
couple who use Vaseline as a sexual aid—they put it on the door-knob
to stop the kids getting into the bedroom!

verandah, there's a light on the . . . but nobody's home

Used to describe a thick person who gives the appearance of having
some intelligence.

walloper

wake-up, to be a . . . to

To recognise an attempt to deceive or to be totally aware of the situation.

Walla Walla, further behind than

To be at an almost impossible disadvantage. Walla Walla was a famous pacer who won many races despite insurmountable handicaps.

walloper

Derogatory term for policeman.

wanger

The penis.

wash-up, the final

Gold-mining term meaning the end result.

Watsons, to bet like the

To bet aggressively. Originating from the Watson brothers (noted gamblers).

weak as piss

Description of ineffectual person or watered-down beer.

welter, making a . . . of it

Taking excessive advantage of a situation.

Werribee duck, in more shit than a

To be in deep trouble. Werribee Sewage Farm is situated in Victoria with an abundance of bird life.

whinger

One who complains incessantly.

whiskers, a punch in the

Vulgar term for sexual intercourse. (See **spearing the bearded clam.**)

White Lady

A mixture of methylated spirits, a dash of boot polish and iodine. Hold the olive, barman! (Not available at your favourite bar!)

white, the man in

In Aussie Rules—the umpire.

whizzer

Male or female genitalia.

whizz off

Depart. People whizz off on holidays, to lunch, to the pub and so on. I'm going to whizz off to the funny farm as soon as I've finished this!

wombat

A frequent male fornicator. He eats, roots, shoots and leaves.

Woodser, Jimmy

Bloke who drinks alone in a pub (see also **drinking with the flies**).

wood, to have the . . . on

To hold an advantage over your opponent with knowledge of his weaknesses.

woofers

Not only found in stereo speakers but also wandering around the streets. Dogs.

Woolloomooloo uppercut

Woolloomooloo uppercut

This'll make your eyes water—a kick in the testicles!

working off a dead horse

Working off a debt.

worries, no

An integral part of the laconic, Aussie attitude. A common expression of re-assurance no matter how adverse the situation.

wrap, to give a big . . . to

To be full of praise for someone or something.

wrestling, open air

What Aussie Rules fan call Rugby League—also known as mobile wrestling and cross-country wrestling.

Yarra

yabber

Idle chatter (see **parliament**).

yatchtie

A yachtsman, of course!

yack, all . . . and no yakker

All talk and no work. (See **parliament** again!)

yack, having a

Having a chat or gossip.

Yarra

A seemingly insane person. Originating from mental asylum situated in Yarra Bend in Victoria.

yike

A serious disagreement or argument.

yow, to keep

To keep watch.

feeding time at the zoo

zoo, feeding time at the
Expression used to describe a mob demolishing free food or drink.

Z-z-z-z-z-z
The sound made by reader after completing this book!